SHORT TERM RENTAL SUCCESS STORIES FROM THE EDGE VOLUME 2

Igniting Your Community in the Sharing Economy

2018 EDITION

M2 Asset Publishing, Inc.

Av. Mutualismo 1321

Independencia 22055 Tijuana, B.C. Mexico

All rights reserved. No part of this book may be reproduced, stored in a retrieval system or transmitted in any form or by any means - electronic or mechanical, photocopying, recording, or any other - except for brief quotations in printed reviews, without prior permission from the publisher.

Success Stories from the Edge (series and concepts), T.E.R.M. ®2008 and their Logo and Marks are Trademarks of Matt Malouf.

Although the author, co-authors and publisher have made every effort to ensure the accuracy and completeness of information contained in this book, we assume no responsibility for errors, inaccuracies, omissions, or any inconsistency herein. The information in this book is sold without warranty, either express or implied.

ISBN: 9781719825665

2018 Edition

Publication Date: August 2018

Version 1 © Copyright 2018 - M2 Asset Publishing, Inc.

To my beautiful, loving and supportive spouse Gladys, whose support and strength inspire me every day. To my kids who make life meaningful and worth living, thank you Andrew, Edward, Roxxane, Cally, Elon. Also, an extended thank you to the rest of my family and friends whose support and encouragement are appreciated everyday even if that list is too long to mention here, you know who you are. Love you guys (and gals).

Forward

We face countless decisions daily. We all do. Many are small and trite and meaningless. But there are a few that are meaningful and can either move one forward or retard growth. How do we make these decisions? We use heuristics (as defined by Wikipedia):

A heuristic technique, often called simply a heuristic, is any approach to problem solving, learning, or discovery that employs a practical method not guaranteed to be optimal or perfect, but sufficient for the immediate goals. Where finding an optimal solution is impossible or impractical, heuristic methods can be used to speed up the process of finding a satisfactory solution. Heuristics can be mental shortcuts that ease the cognitive load of making a decision.

So, we tend to do what we've done in the past because that is our internal guideline of what has worked. However, is that the MOST OPTIMAL way to perform?

What if your natural response (like most humans) tends to lean towards "conservative" or "risk averse" and therefore, you are missing tremendous opportunities?

The first step, I believe is to surround oneself with people who are trying new things; learning and making mistakes. But making forward progress. This smaller 'tribe' of folks is very optimistic. Which is also quite encouraging and comforting. Even in the face of adversity, mistakes, losses, and other "bad things" they remain upbeat and continue to try, iterating, until they get it right. And, eventually, they do! But, most importantly, they are changing their outlook in life. Suddenly, their heuristics are no longer risk averse. They are open to new ideas and opportunities. And, they hone an ability to take small risks which gradually over time, begin to shift their life and lifestyles.

Matt Malouf has put together a collection of such contributors in this book. It is well worth reading as everyone shows vulnerability and fear. And, how they personally recognized this fear (which is the first step) and then consciously expressed a desire to change.

I'm thrilled that I've created a "safe" community on Facebook, YouTube and through our online membership for like-minded ordinary people looking to stretch their wings and experiment in a safe zone with guidance, friendship, mentoring and a growth orientation.

Read their stories (please) and see what resonates with you.

Are you interested in growing? Are you scared (it's highly likely you feel anxious about taking the next step or find reasons not to do it. "The time is not right. I don't have the capital. I don't have time. I heard of someone who lost a lot of money." Whatever the excuse is, it doesn't matter - it resonates with you personally and prohibits you from moving forward. It is real.

Come hang out on the other side of the fence. One where we view opportunities with optimism and instead of avoiding risk, we begin to embrace it, slowly, methodically, holding your hand throughout. Baby steps. I personally have achieved the success I have by having a divergent viewpoint. Risk is my friend because everyone else eschews risk, it is mispriced. And, like being the "House" at the casino, if I take enough calculated, smart risks, at the right time, and price it correctly, over time, I win. My heuristic that I lean on with every decision is to accept risk and actively seek it out. I'm not a daredevil. I'm not foolish. But, I am self-aware that I can grow personally and professionally faster and further by embracing calculated risk. And, once I realized that, my life changed.

I encourage you to read this book. Join our free Facebook Group (https://str.university/community), subscribe to our free YouTube channel (@struniversity) to learn how to monetize the roof over your very own head and get started with minimal risk. We'd love to have you and help you grow!

I leave you with a quote from "The Greatest":

> *"He who is not courageous enough to take risks will accomplish nothing in life."*
>
> Muhammad Ali

Best,
Richard Fertig
Founder of Short Term Rental University

Introduction

Becoming just 1% better every week will drastically change your outlook and lifestyle. ***Short Term Rental Success Stories from the Edge*** is a breakthrough in the short term rental market. Rather than publishing a 50,000-word treatise on how you can make all this money on short term rentals and travel the globe on 4 hours of work a week, we went in the opposite direction. We reached out and found some of the best thought leaders around, action takers who took a leap of faith to make their dreams come true through commitment, hard work and action.

Each of our experts has made an art form of achieving their success in the short term rental market by building and igniting a powerful community to support their success. Each has written a powerful and moving chapter allowing you some insight into their heart and soul about igniting the power of community (however you define it) and come out on the other side better. A better host(ess), a better guest, a better entrepreneur, a better family member or friend.

Each of our authors has agreed to lay it all on the line and hold nothing back. Every one of them has made a commitment to your success by sharing their thoughts and experiences. Should you find a particular author or authors who impact you, please feel free to reach out to them through their contact information provided at the end of their chapter.

Here's my simple advice on how to successfully get the most out of reading this book... Commit to one chapter a day.

That's all folks. Each chapter should not take more than about 15-20 minutes to read. A chapter is easy to do, but it's also easy NOT to do. Which is why we ask your commitment. Each author and contributor took time out of their busy lives to commit. They took time away from their business, from their families to commit to expanding the human experience by sharing their trials and tribulations. They took a leap of faith, a keyboard and poured their heart and soul out there.

Here's how I define commitment… Doing what you said you would do because you said you would do it, through thick and thin, regardless of the odds and distresses.

If you're willing to give up on any excuses and commit to just one simple chapter a day, you will begin to see a shift in your short term rental business, a shift in your attitude, a shift in your life. We all face challenges and adversity in life, it happens, especially in your short term rental business. We cannot survive yet thrive alone, which is why the common theme in this Volume is *Community*. Community is so important. There are so many ways to define community and we have a few great stories of how these entrepreneurs built and used community to achieve a breakthrough in their short term rental business to then improve their lives.

What did I do to go from nothing to achieve a wonderful life full of love, opportunity and hope? I took small steps every day towards my perceived goals, and when those goals changed, I adjusted myself and my thinking to meet the challenges ahead. Most importantly, I drew support and inspiration from those around me (my community) who overcame similar issues to design a fulfilling life worth living, a life that makes a difference.

I would also like to thank every author who contributed their valuable stories and experiences to this project. Thank you so much Crystal L Reed, Zack Scriven, Kevin Borgersen, Lynel Johnson. Without your hard work and leap of faith this wouldn't even be possible.

Let me be the first to say thank you from the bottom of my heart for helping me mark something off my bucket list and for picking up this book. Now is the time to get committed, to conquer and crush those fears to be the success we all know we were meant to be.

-*Matt Malouf*

Table of Contents

You Are the Company You Keep 11
A Rising Tide Lifts All Ships 17
Community: Shrinking the World One Suitcase at a Time 24
Bone Headed Idiots 33
Igniting the Power of Community: Airbnb 39
AFTERWORD 49

You Are the Company You Keep

By Crystal L Reed

Community: Neighborhood, Area, District, Village, Commune, People, Group, Network, etc. Aren't those descriptive words about community beautiful and powerful?

A community can be made up of many components: physically, organizationally, socially, professionally, friend or familial relationships. I'm a part of many communal groups and activities but the one I'm most proactive and loyal to is my familial community.

Without a good family community nucleus, there's no cheerleader, no sounding board, no ear to bend and if in a real desperate situation, no couch to crash on or money to borrow. If there's no family, success becomes harder to define and share.

When the economy took a downward turn in 2007 a lot of people moved back in with parents, family and friends due to loss of income, loss of home or inability to find gainful employment. Single mothers like me relied on community (as we always have) to help with overall care for our children. When there's no community (village) to fall back on, it's even harder to manage the day-to-day. With a community's support, childcare, transportation, sports involvement, less days off work to stay home with a sick child or attending a school field trip all becomes possible.

In business, it's called networking but it's truly just another form of community. Networking is a close-knit group of individuals that make a concerted effort to avail themselves to others in need of information, referrals, loans, contacts, locations, connections and introductions. The community is the hub and the networks and networkers are the spokes that create extended communities. Anyone that claims to be self-made should really take time to re-evaluate each strategic move and episode to realize that there was community involvement to be credited in the machinations of creating who they are and what they have obtained and achieved.

True, there can be those that are not directly involved in close knit communities and may very well operate as lone wolves but, directly or indirectly there was a collective with a support system that was used as a resource to further an individual's endeavors, even if it was ancestrally. We all stand on the shoulders of others whether we admit it or not.

At the very core of my being is the DNA of generations before me that put me in the right place at the right time to create the type of communities I would need when I needed them; the type of communities I would give and take from. To be able to call upon my Village as a single mother when I had a need or to be able to reach out to my business Network when I need to accomplish a task are beyond priceless.

I grew up in Philadelphia in a neighborhood that was the epitome of community. This idyllic environment was typical of that location and era. As children, we played outside in the summer months until the street lights came on. We roamed and explored as much of the entire neighborhood as we dared. We played in the middle of the street and back driveways. The adults in the community, other parents, shop operators, city workers, teachers, clergy…everyone, watched over us like we were their very own. In some instances, they disciplined us if they caught us out of line and then sent us home to our parents with a message and the assurance of being disciplined again for having been involved in shenanigans in the first place. That community of years gone by created lifelong friendships, relationships, marriages, children and a sense of belonging. It was an example of an era and environment that embraced the community ethos.

Several years ago, I moved with a company from California to the Midwest. Fortunately, I was not the only employee from the company to move and it was a little easier creating a close community of co-workers and friends. They not only could relate to the California life-style and culture, but it caused us to rely on and be supportive of each throughout our tenure because we gravitated toward each other with a mutual bond. It was nice to have the sense of community and support as a woman in her mid-twenties and away from my blood family for the first time. As time marches on so does the makeup of community. Some remain extremely close, others journey on. Communities ebb and flow and evolve over time...the old must make way for the new or different.

Fast forward to living in California (for the second time) and the term *Community* is loosely held because it's a very transient state, especially if you live close to a military installation. People don't get to know each other in kindergarten and create the interwoven bond that lasts a lifetime once created by the east coast way of life. People don't stay in a neighborhood, raise their children and remain rooted in one location until the mortgage is paid off and retire there. Homes are not designed to have neighbors sit on the front porch and chat or watch each other's children play outside. Garages are in the front of homes to save precious real estate footage, so you are forced to drive directly in and out of your property, rarely engaging other neighbors. You can go for days...weeks even and no one will know if you reside there any longer, let alone, know if you are dead or alive. It's not conducive to chatting across the fence while hanging laundry to dry in the sweet summer sun to secure that fresh linen smell. It doesn't promote block parties, children walking to school together in a massive group from kindergarten to high school – they take buses out of the area to attend a 'better' school. People relocate frequently due to employment, family obligations, deployment or because the high cost of living has finally become too much to bear.

The only way I see to compensate for this bygone era is to cultivate the community you wish to be a part of. A community does not have to consist of only blood relatives or a neighborhood. As we age, mature and evolve, family becomes those that are closest to us in our inner circle, those you know are in your corner, those you can depend on...ride or die type folk.

As adults, it's not as though you can go outside and ask people to come and play. Therefore, you have to work a little harder to develop new and lasting connections who make up your community. This is particularly true for military people who relocate often. The only difference I see in this scenario is in the Skydiving community. My STR mainly houses skydivers because my home is located very close to the #1 drop zone in the world, Perris, California. When I talk with my guests or go over to the drop zone to watch them jump, I get to see the camaraderie, support and bond that the skydivers have and (in some instances) develop quickly (like on the way up in the air or out of the plane). They often see each other only a few times a year and at other drop zones throughout the world. They also meet up to participate in formation events and competitions and jump as cohesive units even though they may have just met. They look out for each other's safety as far as equipment is concerned, share food and jump stories. The Skydiving community is ever evolving and fascinating and I enjoy getting to know them. I've been afforded another opportunity to create and expand a unique community by operating my short term rental business through the use of various sharing economy platforms such as Airbnb, HomeAway, etc. Making fast friends and getting involved in your surroundings takes a lot of extra work, but it can be accomplished if you really desire to fortify a community base that is supportive of you and vice versa.

I don't personally believe we were created to live a solitary life. I believe we are here to help and support each other in many areas of our lives. I believe paths cross for a time, reason and season – some seasons lasting longer than others. We are here to teach and to learn...from each other. One drop of water can make a ripple in a pond, but we have to be willing to allow ourselves the opportunity to make that ripple.

My personal community, la Familia, the fambam, my rock – they remain solid and true; blood related and otherwise.

CRYSTAL L REED

Crystal (Crys) has been in the Marketing & Sales arena for over 25 years. She has worked for H.J. Heinz Co., StarKist Foods, Inc., Heinz Pet Products, Mountain View Community Church of Temecula and KinderCare Learning Centers. She was born and raised in Philadelphia, PA, and in her last year of high school, moved to Los Angeles, CA. After college, she embarked upon her career with Heinz and relocated to Cincinnati, OH/Newport, KY until 2000. Crys then returned to Southern California where she currently resides and operates business endeavors which include BCC - Small Business Management Services (Business Concierge, Virtual Admin & Social Media Support, Event & Networking Coordinator), A Suite Collaboration (Hospitality Services on Short Term Rental Platforms), Crystal's Jewel Persuasion (specializing in Medical Alert & Regular Bracelets Male/Female) and Jamboree of Unstoppable Networking Women (Networking, Training, Education and Celebration of Women Entrepreneurs) and Public Speaker/Motivator/Encourager. Her deepest passion is mentoring and coming along side women of all ages to encourage and promote them during their personal journeys and entrepreneurial endeavors. She loves comedy and romantic movies, dancing like no one is watching, car dancing, singing loud and off-key in bumper to bumper traffic and throwing her head back in knee-slapping laughter. She is currently in a new phase of her life's journey...empty-nester and she is opening her heart, life and home to all of Life's and Love's possibilities.

= = = = = = = = = = =

CONTACT:

CL Reed
Email: asuitecollaboration@gmail.com
Twitter: @asuitecollab
Instagram: @asuitecollaboration
Facebook: @ASUITEC

BCC | SMALL BUSINESS MANAGEMENT SERVICES

951.777.0255
P.O. Box 141
Murrieta, California 92564-0141
bccsbms@gmail.com
www.BeCrysClear.net
http://www.Facebook.com/BCC– Small Business Management Services

A Rising Tide Lifts All Ships

by Zack Scriven

As you are sitting and reading this, I am sitting here talking into a microphone. Over the course of this chapter, I am excited to talk to you about my Airbnb experience. I'm not a very good writer or reader, and this is my first time being a published author, but here I am. As for being an Airbnb host, I just jumped in and did it. What I really want you to get out of this story is that it's all about how I developed a supportive community through my short term rental adventures and how this community that I have built has changed my life in so many ways.

The way we started down this path is pretty unique. My girlfriend, Mary, and I went from renting a spare bedroom on Airbnb in our home to being Airbnb real estate investors. We didn't initially intend on being Airbnb hosts as a "thing." In 2015, I had heard about the sharing economy platform from a friend using it to travel and downloaded it. I was really interested in the hosting and business aspect of it. I went through the process of listing my room but didn't published it for about a year. I was interested in seeing how much money we could earn and what going through the process of being a host would be like.

In 2016, Mary and I officially welcomed our first guest as Airbnb hosts in the spare bedroom of our home, who happened to be my mother. Let me explain. My mom lives in Arizona and was traveling to California for work. In an effort to save her company money, instead of staying at a hotel, she was staying with family. Her company was kind enough to reimburse us $50 for each night she stayed with family. I suggested instead of her company writing a check, "Why don't I just list it on Airbnb? Then your company can book it through there and it will be official." We did that several times and that worked out great!

At that point our listing was active, and we received our first reservation request from someone other than my mom! Mary and I discussed the request, or rather I tried over and over to convince her that we should accept the request and give it a shot. We finally decided (she caved) that we would try out hosting someone other than my mom, someone who was basically a stranger to us. Her name was Lauren. It was her first time staying as a guest on Airbnb too! We will never forget that initial feeling of nervousness and excitement of hosting a stranger for the first time. It was awesome in the end because she was the nicest person we could have asked for! She was social, but not overly needy. She cleaned up after herself and made herself at home, like she was family.

At first, Mary and I decided that we were going to host only women and only on the weekends because our daughter, Zoë was only a few months old at the time. Letting strangers into our home was a major consideration. However, we quickly acclimated to the feeling and before we knew it the "only girls and only on the weekend" rule was thrown out the window and we were hosting guests back to back!

We couldn't have taken advantage of this opportunity at a better time. Mary was still out of work on maternity leave, so the extra income of renting our spare bedroom really helped us through that time. The income started growing over a few months. It got to the point where it not only helped subsidize our income, but really help us flourish financially! Paying our bills suddenly got a lot easier.

After about 8 months of hosting we started to look for investment properties to purchase. We were still renting the spare bedroom at our home that got us started on this adventure. This was nice, but we really wanted to own real estate. We decided that we would look for a property that we could purchase to rent on Airbnb. Our backup plan was that if Airbnb didn't work out it was a home we would be willing to move into ourselves.

Within the first year we put an offer on and purchased a two-bedroom condo that was right down the street. In that first year of hosting we made over $20,000. Being Airbnb hosts made a big impact on our finances and gave us the confidence to buy a real estate investment for the purposes of Airbnb.

Unfortunately, the two bedroom condo didn't work out as planned. The Home Owners Association (HOA) was against rentals for less than 30 days. The condo was in a brand new development area and rules were getting established. First, they sent a couple letters stating that they were aware of the short term rentals that were happening and that it was against the rules, so we compromised with finding Airbnb renters who wanted to stay 30 days or longer. During this time, it was amazing to be able to turn to the STR community for advice and support. Many people had gone through the challenges we were facing, and we were able to learn from their experience.

It is pretty humbling being 25 years old and owning real estate. Airbnb was that platform which in many ways got Mary and me to that point. I did pull out a bit of money from my Roth IRA for the down payment. I looked at the real estate investment as a way of diversification from the stock market. It really was a good opportunity for me to buy. That's one of the reasons why I liked the Roth IRA because I knew I could use some of the principal funds without any taxes or any penalties to put towards my first home. It wasn't a loan, so I don't need to pay it back!

At this point we continued to grow the business. We joined an online community called, *Short Term Rental Secrets* which then became *Short Term Rental University* (STRU). At that time the Facebook Group was over 6,000 people. At the time of writing this it's over 10,000 people of short term rental hosts. The founder of the community is Richard Fertig. He is a serial entrepreneur and Airbnb Guru. I really was drawn to the positive and supportive nature of the community. There were so many active members posting photos, engaging in the comments, and providing value.

This engagement in the community really helped Mary and me to stay focused on our goals of being great hosts and great business owners too!

Joining this community was really crucial in my personal entrepreneurial journey. Not just for learning Airbnb tips, but for learning what Richard himself was doing. He wasn't just an Airbnb Host, he was building an online community and business! At face value he was teaching Airbnb tips, but really what I learned from him is how to be an entrepreneur, how to build my own online community, how to make valuable video content and how he pushed through when he only got 100 subscribers in the first month of his YouTube Channel.

I became very active within the STRU Facebook group. I was posting comments, posting photos. I started building a reputation within the community. One of my posts sharing how much I made within the first year ($20k) went viral on Facebook. Richard was coming to Los Angeles for a local meetup and asked if I would be on the first episode of the STRU podcast. Of course, I accepted, and the experience was enlightening. I met Richard and his Videographer Charles Hurley at their Airbnb in Venice Beach, CA.

Shortly after that initial podcast I started going live to the Facebook group to say hello and summarize some of what was going on in the STR community. I also started doing more YouTube live streams. I organized a couple peer listing review webinars. I started my own podcast. I really was trying to learn from what Richard did himself and use that to build my own support community in my own way.

As a crucial part of my journey being a part of that Facebook group. I started reaching out to various people and businesses that had products or services for Airbnb hosts. I started featuring these companies using live video and content posts. I would be completely honest and open about how I felt about their service which I would negotiate to get for free. I was like a micro influencer within the community.

For example, Danny from *Optimize My Airbnb* has a service where he will go in and rewrite your Airbnb listing description. I proposed to him that we do a live stream where we conference call and screen share and he rewrites my listing live. The exposure within the community brought him additional clients! And I got a $250 free service out of the deal! The concept worked in reality!

I also featured Karen and Mercedes from *One Chic Retreat*. They gave me a really great discount on their Interior Design Services. They helped us redecorate the condo and stage it properly for photos. I documented the process. I did live streams of before, during, and after. Believe it or not they also got leads and referrals from the efforts. I was building a support community of my very own filled with like-minded successful entrepreneurs learning their tips and secrets to success along the way.

So why am I telling you this? Using Airbnb to build a community was how I boot-strapped my way into entrepreneurship and then into home ownership. Building a supportive, like-minded community helped me realize that people will pay me for my talent with video. Helping me to develop and grow the concept that I can get paid doing what I love. The whole experience was a confidence-builder and proof of concept. I kept trying new things and growing little by little. This eventually grew to the point where I quit my engineering career to pursue a career in content creation and influencer marketing full time. It's been nearly three months and a wild ride so far, but I couldn't be happier.

It's rather ironic that I'm writing a chapter for a book on Airbnb success, yet I am not actually an Airbnb host at the moment, but that is my story. Airbnb played a crucial role in getting Mary and me to be homeowners. It also played a huge role in helping me find my passion for entrepreneurship, video content creation, building a community, and marketing. We really enjoyed our time being Airbnb hosts because we met a lot of amazing people. We had a lot of fun hosting and the money was good too. We would become hosts again in a heartbeat if the opportunity presents itself but for now our focus is elsewhere. So that's really how my Airbnb story was so crucial to my overarching long-term story and I really think that it could play a crucial part in your story. Just give it a shot. Build your own community and see where it takes you. Life is a journey and I recommend that you just jump in and make it happen like I am doing. I think you will find yourself quite surprised at how supportive people can be when given the opportunity to contribute to a community that they can believe in. Believe in yourself above all else. See you on the other side.

Zack Scriven

Zack Scriven is a 25-year-old father, fiancé, real estate investor, and entrepreneur. He grew up in Upland, California where he gained experience at an early age in the Control System Integration industry working for his parents' company. By the age of 21 he left college to become the Lead System Integrator. Shortly after he purchased the company from his mother and was a solo business owner for several years.

Zack has a passionate and outgoing personality. For example, he met his fiancée, Mary Woods, a flight attendant while she was at work. The two instantly hit it off and became partners. After a year of dating Zack and Mary  were blessed with a baby on the way. Zack took this life changing event as an opportunity to better himself, his career, and his family.

He closed down his company and took a job at a system integration firm.

While the job had its perks and he was learning rapidly, again being in a new environment around new people, Zack's entrepreneurial itch began to grow. Shortly after Mary and Zack welcomed their daughter Zoë into the world they began welcoming guests from all over the world into their home. Zack began to scratch again his entrepreneurial itch by starting an Airbnb business with Mary out of their spare bedroom.

What first started as extra income to support the couple through their maternity leave turned quickly into a thriving business and the two purchasing a rental property. Zack became an active member in the Short Term Rental University Community of hosts. This not only helped guide them into becoming successful hosts and business owners but also uncovered a hidden passion of Zack's for video content creation and community building.

======

CONTACT:
Follow Zack's Daily Adventures at:
https://www.zackscriven.com/

Community: Shrinking the World One Suitcase at a Time

by Lynel Johnson

Initially, finding out you're going on a trip means you're going to do something fun in a place that isn't "Home." We figure out what it is we want to do when we arrive, we plan and pack our appropriate gear and clothing and we start counting down the days on the calendar.

When I was young going on a trip meant Dad would put our family of four into the station wagon and drive us Up North to The Cabin. In Minnesota, Up North is definitely a place, it's the place where people go to The Cabin. "The Cabin", which is what we would call whatever cabin we would end up renting in summer was always on a lake, so swimsuits and life vests were probably packed first. Other gear would include summer clothes for playtime and warm sweatshirts and jeans to wear around a bonfire in the evening. Memories were sure to be made. The hard-sided red cooler, filled with all kinds of delicious summer salads mom would have prepared, was a staple on our trips. It had a place of honor in the back of the car near the top, so Dad could put ice in it at our first possible stop and beverages would be easily accessible for thirsty girls. And last, but especially not least, were the fishing rods. Dad would gingerly thread them from the back and set them carefully near the neck rest of our seats with a stern warning to "Watch the tips!". Although I knew he didn't want the tips broken, I was a little more concerned about those hooks hanging off the lures. Once we were all in the car and the doors slammed shut, Dad would say a quick little one sentence prayer of safety and almost giddily start the car.

That was it. The four of us, our own little organic community; Mom, Dad, my sister, Esther and me driving north with the trees getting taller and greener and the skies becoming more and more blue as it starts to dance on the waves of many of the 10,000 lakes we'd pass, until we arrived at that one, The One, "The Lake."

Before a trip we know the what and the where and the when. That's what we research. Where will we go? What can we do when we get there? Then we check our schedules and calendars freeing up time to be away from normal life. We make arrangements for normal life to continue or pause while we're away.

After a trip the stories include the what and the where, but they almost always also include a surprising "We", the Who for which we had not planned. The 'We' consists of the others that you bump up against while out and about who become part of your story. But a select few of the 'We' become part of your community.

In my memory our community grew during those camping trips. We would inevitably meet the guy at the bait shop or, as I remember it, the couple who lived in the cabin next door. She was always on the deck doing some handiwork, stitching. An older gal who would smile and give cookies to two little barefooted Rugrats enjoying a week of summer somewhere else. In the evening we would all share stories together and I would listen to my parents laugh at old stories not realizing we were making a new story of our own.

I might be able to come up with the town name of that hosted summer trip, but as far as the old couple's names go.... All of those summer trip experiences have taught me that community can be for seasons – they may not always last forever. After a while Up North wasn't so far anymore. My mental map had grown, and the world shrunk, just a bit.

"A dream job that is continuing to come true in my life is Hosting the Traveler. Being able to combine my love of travel with the excitement of meeting new people from different places mesh well together as a short term rental host."

-Lynel Johnson

My husband was reading an online article to me the first time I heard about Airbnb. It seemed like a crazy concept of having people you don't know pay to stay in your home or spare room.

We have all seen that meme that says 20 years ago we were told not to jump in a stranger's car and don't talk to people online. And now we summon strangers online to pick us up in their cars and stay in their homes.

Our family loves to have people over. Getting to know others over a meal or a board game leads to lots of laughs and friendships. Sharing experiences with others is the stuff of tomorrows' stories. These experiences grow into golden precious moments in our minds. And the people to whom they belong become our community. Our people.

Our first experience as paying guests in a rental home came in 2015. We stayed in a 10th floor apartment just blocks from Copacabana beach in Rio de Janeiro, Brazil. Now I don't know if it was the salt water in the air, the sounds of the music on the street or just experiencing life on another hemisphere but it was exciting dragging my bags to that apartment. We had someone else's apartment all to ourselves for our whole stay! To look out of the windows and see the views as the locals gave me perma-grin.

Visiting a city shows us places, the sights, the draw; maybe a beach or Museum or monument. Maybe we will do some shopping and step into a City's stores. But visiting someone's community it's just a few degrees different than their city. This takes on a different perspective. It is more about the people, the store clerk the coffee shop waitress, the street vendor you pass on the way to the sights. In this case the host of the home we rented became part of our community, my friend - part of my story.

A couple of summers later we were celebrating our 25th wedding anniversary, my husband, Tim decided to take me to Italy! A mixture of Hotel variety and Airbnb listings became our accommodations. Any time I can get away and stay somewhere else experiencing a new place - I am all in! Italy is beautiful, and we marveled at the beauty! In the hotels where we stayed there was a comfort of familiarity. We understood the front desk; key use and it was fun to point out the differences between the hotels' locations. We have stayed in short term rental accommodations twice. While there was less familiarity, there was much more growth from the new experience. Experiencing the home as a local was very rewarding. Knowing the host was just a phone call and the next door down calmed any fear of needing help. Starting the washing machine proved tricky, as surprising as it is for us to imagine, not everything is written in English, even with a helpful app we were unsuccessful. Super Host to the rescue! Turns out it just needed a reboot. The ol' unplug and re-plug did the trick. Before we knew it, our clothes were having their first afternoon on a clothesline overlooking Riomaggiore, Cinque Terra. Oh, you want to go there. Find Paulo on Airbnb and tell him Lynel sent you.

Brazil is now more than a very large country on the other side of a globe to us. We know its' sights and sounds and smells. We know its people. The distance to Brazil is now measured in flight hours not miles. It is now part of my mental map and story.

After having some experience as a guest in an Airbnb the idea of hosting became very attractive to me. What if I could be the one who handed out a key and welcomed someone into my city? We currently have long term rental properties, but there really isn't a draw for vacationers here so it doesn't make sense to turn it into a short term rental. Twenty minutes north of here there are many draws; a community on the Mississippi River, multiple colleges, churches that host weddings and two Convention Centers. There is plenty of activity there and I decided I would love to introduce people to that space.

The antique looking little homes in that city were just screaming to be purchased, decorated and put on a short term rental platform for anyone to find. The real estate market place platform, Zillow became my new friend – an obsession really. Our quest began. I would find myself logging on every day to see if there might be a house that fit my criteria in the neighborhood most convenient to host travelers. My virtual map of the city became riddled with the heart symbol used to select listings as a 'favorited' home that I wanted to tour. In the end it came down to just one, the one I called, "A home from a simpler time."

Not long after my quest began some of my sisters-in-law, nieces and I decided to take a girls' trip to Texas and visit other nieces. You can bet your wannabe cowboy boots that I arranged short term rental accommodations for this trip. We rented a whole home that was outfitted to look very Tex-ish. We wanted that hoedown feel! It was so exciting when everyone piled into the house with their bags and started exploring. The Women picked out their bedrooms and remarked about the furnishings and décor. We ogled and enjoyed the fun treats that were left out for us and settled in for our stay. It wasn't long before we were picking each other's' brains about how we could make this work in Minnesota. Months earlier, Tim and I had put an offer on a four-unit building (Quad) near a hockey arena that I had dreams of turning into a rental to host sports fans. The offer fell through, but the wheels were still turning. We all have our niches and decorating is not mine, but my Sis in law Julie – now she's got an eye and she was there in Texas to catch the vision! On our third day back in Minnesota she and I were touring homes with a realtor found a home and made an offer. Six days later an offer was accepted. Eight weeks later we closed on the house, January 5, 2018. By the end of the next month it was listed on Airbnb and two weeks later we had our first guests. It was all so exciting, I didn't know what to do with myself once the house was up and running, doing what we hoped it would do – providing a warm, comfortable, beautiful space for guests to stay while visiting Minnesota.

While Julie was busily decorating I was tasked with learning how to run this place the best way. For this, I went to my go-to helper for all things unknown – YouTube. It did not disappoint. It happened to be perfect timing for finding Richard Fertig, Founder of Short Term Rental University, a Super Host who was teaching tried and true steps on what to do to get your home ready and running on short term rental platforms like Airbnb and HomeAway. It was obviously time for a fresh notebook. My to-do list was growing and so was my knowledge of a new business. Just weeks after starting to devour all that he had to teach, he mentioned a new start up course to take business to a more granular level, digging into all the aspects of this work. The day of online enrollment my information was in their system and I knew I was on my way to a deeper understanding of all I needed to know. A Facebook group was started for all of us eager learners. I popped in to see what was available. One month before we even closed on the house a shift happened at my computer. This tool, used so often to research and learn, became a two-way street. A new understanding of community came into view, and my world got smaller again. Here's this guy that I have watched repeatedly, posing questions and answering others – answering me! Many others like myself were now not just watching but interacting. This resource turned into many friendship relationships. We have common goals and we encourage each other. They all cheered me on when my house was listed on Airbnb. I now understood the excitement of others in my short term rental community once they took the leap of faith and listed their properties. Sometimes we've had to wrestle with figuring out best practices in certain areas. Here is this group of people, two-dimensional friends, who understand my questions, fears and my joys. We challenge, encourage and guide each other as we learn to host our guests and grow our businesses the best possible way.

Someday, I will pack a suitcase and meet some of my new community members, in three dimension – we understand each other. These relationships have formed a community. Broadening my community is shrinking the world one suitcase at a time.

If you have some sort of business ideas maybe you want to go into real estate or take the risk of running a short-term rental, let me encourage you to step out of your comfort zone. Find those people who are doing the things that intrigue you and learn from them. You may have some thoughts and ideas that can help others in their business and helping each other will strengthen you as a person. There's a sort of confidence that surprisingly sneaks in when you make the decision to take a risk, a calculated healthy life changing risk.

I named my company *Feel Free* and topped off the logo with a hospitable pineapple. I want my guests to feel welcomed. I think all hosts want their guests to be comfortable and ultimately to feel at home. If you're feeling like you have that tug of interest, it doesn't really matter what stage of life you're in, and you can make hosting part of your resume too. You can start small with a room in your house. Maybe you have another level in your house you would like to use to host. Figure out what your strengths and weaknesses are and find the people or the resources you can use to either supplement or strengthen that weakness in yourself and build your own community.

It might seem like a crazy notion to purchase a home that you can decorate and use to host others. There are a lot of opportunities to join in the real estate investing pool. Take a risk. We did!

LYNEL JOHNSON

Lynel Johnson is a happily married mother-of-three, raising her family in her home state of Minnesota. Early in their marriage she worked as a flight attendant propelling her love of travel to new heights.

A few years back, with children heading off to college, the Johnsons invested in rental property, thus providing Lynel a new job as property manager. She really enjoys meeting her tenants' needs while keeping the locations in great shape.

Early 2018 saw the purchase of a single-family home to be used as a short-term rental. *Feel Free B&B* has become a great place to host new friends from all over the world.

Recently Tim and Lynel returned home from Brazil where they did community work with friends in underserved neighborhood. They met up with their two Brazilian exchange "daughters" who helped as their interpreters.

Recently, Tim and Lynel added a 20 unit apartment building expanding their rental portfolio to 39 doors.

In her free time, she likes to play games with friends and family laughing or cackling out loud, make colorfully decorated sugar cookies and research her family's genealogy. She's always game for a flight somewhere new with family and old friends - meeting new friends all over the planet.

There's so much to learn in this new chapter of life. Never stop growing and never stop loving others.

= = = = = =

CONTACT:

Email: FeelFreeBnB@gmail.com

https://www.airbnb.com/rooms/23378330

Bone Headed Idiots

by Kevin Borgersen

"If you want to be a bone-headed idiot, hang around with bone-headed idiots. If you want to be successful, you must be around successful people."

-Kevin Borgersen

I am not sure who said this quote, or even if I have the wording exact after all these years, but a professor who taught a business class I took in college handed out this quote on a laminated business card that I carried around in my wallet through most of my life until it was eventually lost. It was with me for so long that I didn't need it anymore since I lived my life by this quote and it has become part of me.

When I started off in the business world I always chose to sit with the older successful people on lunch or go out for drinks with them during the off hours. Truly successful people never mind sharing their stories with young hungry individuals and dish out advice if the recipient is hungry enough to devour it. I was hungry, I was driven, I recruited my own mentors, I succeeded in the corporate environment.

I will always fondly remember one gentleman who was higher up the ladder than I was. His wife had passed years earlier, and his children all had families of their own. We became friends of sorts. He, in his 60's and me barely the legal drinking age would get together and play chess. Hours would pass quickly but the conversations were always fantastic. He enjoyed the company while I enjoyed the vast knowledge and experience he freely shared. This gentleman was truly my first mentor, the first person I respected outside of family and teachers, the first member of my community.

Over chess I learned the secret to my success, treat everybody as equals and with respect – regardless of the position somebody held in any given situation since everybody is the same – we are all in this together. The only difference between a CEO and the janitor is the position played on the team. Every person has the same value. I still live by that idea and was able to see eye to eye with all levels thus helping me to recruit more mentors, team members, and productive members of my community. The names and faces of my community changed over time but the people all remained the same- "Successful and Driven". These were the people I was "attracted" to the most.

A person goes through many phases in life and if they want to move forward and achieve goals, they need to build themselves a strong community. A team is the first thing a person should put together when attempting a new venture, new hobby, new spin on life. Build your team, learn as much as you can, gather your friends with the same interest as that which you are getting into and move forward.

The path I walk is winding as my goals change as my life moves forward and these goals are either achieved, failed at, or I have outgrown. My community has changed with each passing goal change and it changed slowly and hardly noticeable. Until a major life altering decision was made, and my entire community was no longer relevant.

When the time came for me to open my own business I was lost. I researched how to do it, I invested my money, opened up my business, and moved forward. As it turned out, it was a very lonely time in my career. I lacked like-minded people to speak to, I lacked people on my level who understood the unique position of owning and running a company, I lacked a community.

I did have my staff who were fantastic and the reason I was able to make money. I had my family and friends who supported me and would help in any way possible when all I had to do was ask. I had my team, but they were only a part of the community I needed. I lacked the community of peers. Then I was invited into what ended up being my favorite community of all time.

Being in children's entertainment, on a regular basis I dealt with all of my suppliers from food to janitorial supplies and everything in between. Some of my suppliers were part of a business networking group that would only allow one type of business to be a member at a time. Example: they only add one accountant and one plumber. I was asked to join and after a two month trial membership they allowed me to be a full member. For the first time, I didn't build my community, I was invited into an existing one.

These small business titans were doing what I was doing by running a small business and experiencing the lonely at the top syndrome. This group gave us peers that we could stand up and to say, "Here is my issue." and 50 people would say "That happened to me and here is what I did." I was at the stage in my life where I wasn't looking at people above me to mentor, I needed the people at my level who could all share experiences and continue to grow as a business and as people.

After many, many years I sold my business and had to leave the collective and I still dream about starting another business with the entire point as being able to join that group again. I miss my peer support community.

"If you want to be a bone-headed idiot, hang around with bone headed idiots."

I believe there are many sides to a person and there is more to life than just work and family. You need to be you and be with friends while you enjoy life so not only do I always hang around with successful people and grow; I hang out with the bone-headed idiots I call friends. I have various communities of friends where each group represents something I am interested in doing.

In some of these groups I am a novice in an activity and in other groups I am the leader of the group and the most experienced. Regardless of where I fall, I am always learning about the activity we are doing and just having fun being a bone-headed idiot. However, I only visit these groups, not live in them. I live in communities of success.

My most important community is obviously my family. I have an extremely supportive and tightly knit family. From my immediate family to my extended family, we stick together. You can't choose your family, but if you raise your kids right and keep everybody happy, the generations will continue to be supportive of each other. I am lucky.

A community is filled with people you interact with, ask questions, learn each other's situation and give advice based on common experiences on the subject.

My wife and I recently decided to venture into the Short Term Rental market. We only knew one person who had success at it and felt confident we could do it. There was one thing missing... a community. With limited knowledge on the subject, and only a single person's experience to draw from and a lack local networking group dedicated to the Short Term Rental subject, I was at a loss on how to build my community.

I decided to do the next best thing. I jumped on the internet to see what was out there. I do not rely on the internet because you don't know how honest people are or what their experience truly is. It's for research only and I use what I learn to decide on my own what is real and worth trying. So online I went.

I watched several different people do a series of videos on various points of view but watching somebody else in a video is not a community and has the same value as a set of encyclopedias that used to sit on my parents' shelf and opened it up to learn a needed fact.

I came across online chat groups on the subject and I finally found my community. It does lack the face-to-face aspect but accomplishes the same thing, you get to learn the other members and gain "friendships" with them. Some people have success in my new ventures category but most of us are just starting out. We are learning this new industry together, sharing our experiences, and growing our community as a whole to the benefit of each member who actively participates. My community has moved to a virtual setting but am getting similar results.

I am still young enough that I still have enough fire in my belly and a brain that thirsts for knowledge. I want to learn new things, achieve goals I still have yet to dream, and grow my personal wealth in both monetary and family value. My community still includes people to help me along, but the majority are made up of people who look to me a mentor or partner. It's time for me to return the favor and be a productive member of another person's community.

While these new members learn from me, I am still learning from my Short Term Rental community.

KEVIN BORGERSEN

Kevin Borgersen was born and raised in New York City where he still resides today. With his wife Linda and two teenage sons Brian and Eric, the family enjoys long road trips, amusement parks, and most of all food festivals. As a serial entrepreneur he has purchased existing businesses, ran startups, and has also closed failing businesses. His best success after leaving a management position in Corporate America was as an independent owner of a children's entertainment facility that won multiple local awards in categories such as "Best Party" and "Best Customer Service"

Eager to try new things, he has also run business from exercise gyms to online sales platforms, has worked in both the corporate and private sectors, and has done everything from piloting an airplane, to SCUBA diving wrecks in some of the oceans of the world.

Kevin and his wife Linda purchased their first Short Term Rental in December 2017 in the Pocono Mountains in Pennsylvania and are currently planning on purchasing their second in a beach vacation community. The plan is to continue to purchase Short Term Rental properties wherever they like to vacation so that when they retire they can flow from one property to their next and enjoy the golden years traveling.

= = = = = =

CONTACT:
Visit Kevin's rental at: https://t.vrbo.io/s85PigKvMM
Kevin Borgersen, Realtor
Herman & Co.
7319 Amboy Rd.
Staten Island, NY 10309
718-757-1384

Igniting the Power of Community: Airbnb

by Matt Malouf

There's no doubt that Airbnb has made travelling easier for people all over the world. I've been a big fan and have made it a habit to use their services every chance I get. To be fair, Airbnb is more than just a mere hospitality service. It is the medium that is connecting people together and provides some unforgettable travel experiences. It is the ease of the app that first introduced me to it and afterwards I just stayed for the convenience. Even after all this time, I recommend the services to any of my friends who want to travel and not worry about finding the right accommodations.

Recently I was thinking, and I realized how Airbnb is doing more than what we think. Just last year I was planning a trip to Italy and wanted it to be the best one ever. But for a change, I wanted to experience the rural life there. It's quite easy to find the right apartments in the main cities (I just had to search on Airbnb), but it was the rural areas that I thought would be a problem.

Social Impact Investing

The idea that emerged in 2007 is the basis of this move by Airbnb. By mobilizing more capital, people across the globe are playing their part in resolving societal problems. Since more capital is needed to tackle the societal and environmental problems, investors are moving their focus towards this issue. There was a time when investors would heavily invest in fossil fuels and other successful industries. They are shifting their attention to other industries.

This gradual increase of interest in social impact investing is definitely going to be a successful surprise in the coming years.

Researchers have estimated that the industry will be worth at least a whopping $650 billion. That's an investment opportunity that should be availed.

Italian Villages

As it turns out, Airbnb had it all covered. In an attempt to increase tourism to the rural parts of the country, Airbnb launched their national project, Italian Villages. It is one of Airbnb's attempts to promote and support rural areas. And the idea has already taken wings.

Everybody loves to travel to bustling cities. I know because I would do the same. Trading one traffic jam for another and it was a tiring experience at times to say the least. It's not that I didn't enjoy the hustle and bustle of the cities I visited, it was just a feeling that something was missing. I loved the crowds and the daily noises of the city but now that the family has grown to two more toddlers, there were times when I would long for a place that was peaceful and quiet. Someplace to slow down and enjoy connecting with nature and people again.

That's the reason I wanted to travel to rural areas, to experience the life there and feel connected to a place that doesn't have air pollution. That's exactly how my search for an Airbnb opportunity in a quaint little village started.

The project is sponsored by The National Association of Italian Municipalities (ANCI) and was developed in collaboration with the Italian Ministry of Culture and Tourism (MiBACT). Over the years, millions of people have visited Italy and continue to do so today. The air of culture, the amazing architecture and of course the people of the country make for an awesome travelling experience. But where most people readily visit the bustling cities, a new trend has tourists looking for more rural options. The motivation behind these changing demographics, as much as I have observed, is the need to get away from the hectic schedule of daily life.

A trip to the rural areas allows people to connect with Mother Nature and explore the less familiar parts of the country. This is the experience that I wanted for my family when we planned to go to Italy.

My search started. What I didn't know at that time was that Airbnb offers this convenient option. I soon discovered the program and needless to say I was ecstatic. It was just what I was looking for and so you can believe my level of excitement at that time.

Italian villages present the perfect opportunity to promote, support and showcase the small Italian towns to travelers. It is a comprehensive platform that allows tourists to select the village of their choice and gain some insights into the unique cultures, traditions and landscapes of the place.

Out of the 40 places that are enrolled in the program, I chose Asolo, a small town in the Northern region. It has mountain settings and the high peaks are the reason it is known as The City of a Hundred Horizons. The place was spectacular. It didn't have the regular features of a city and that's the reason it appealed to me so much. The ease that Airbnb provided me of course cannot outmatch the help that these rural villages are getting from the program.

With some active Airbnb hosts in these areas, the platform is helping people of these rural locations to improve the local economies of these villages. The Airbnb hosts are a way to encourage tourism to these places so that they can work towards a stable economic situation.

Power of Community

Italy isn't the only place where this model can work. With the support of your community, starting such projects in Central America is also a good idea. And for many investors, the financial move has already started paying off well.

When you start a STR (Short term Rental), it makes you a leader and is a promise that good fortune is coming your way. The best way to achieve success in such a model is to leverage the power of the local geographical community. When people have a feeling of fellowship within their community, they are at an advantage. The shared attitudes and interests of the community can be made a reality with a STR. By making winning and long-lasting relationships within the community, people get the power to give back to the community that has provided them with plenty of blessings.

That is the power of community. It connects you and makes you achieve more than you would have while doing it alone. There was a time when I too wasn't a believer. It didn't take long for me to weigh the benefits of a community and become part of a STR. This was the time when my intentions of going solo quickly took a turn.

Here are 6 powerful reasons that convinced me not to do it alone:

1. *Collective Wisdom*

   No one person ever has all of the answers, and regardless of the amount of Googling you may do, consulting with experts is always going to give you better information. Have you ever heard of the saying, "Two heads are better than one."? Yes, it is true and with a community that aims to succeed, the collective wisdom of the people involved is the biggest asset you can ever get.

2. *Pushing Our Limits*

   When working alone it's often too easy to give up when things get hard. I know how I would feel like giving up when there is too much to handle. But it was the power of the community that kept me going, even when the times were hard. By surrounding yourself with others working toward a similar goal or objective, you'll get motivation, support, and friendly competition, as I did, to push yourself just a bit further than you would have done on your own.

3. *Support and Belief*

   Some days those big goals just seem impossible. There were days of total despair, when giving up was the only option left for me, or so I felt. As I learned, you need to lean on your community to get the support you want most. They believe in you—probably more than you believe in yourself. And this unwavering belief in your abilities is one big motivation to continue on with your work.

4. *New Ideas*

   I truly believe that when you are working within a community of like-minded people that the wisdom of crowds is considerably greater than any one person working alone. Our divergent world views and the different lenses we perceive the world through mean that we all approach the exact same problem slightly differently. In the end, it is the pool of different and effective ideas that can help you achieve the shared goal.

5. *Borrowed Motivation*

   There will be days when you'll lack motivation. Don't let it get you down. Doing what needs to be done might seem overwhelming but let your community guide you through this phase. Look around your community and be inspired!

6. *Accountability*

   If you're an uber-responsible person, you may not want to admit to people, especially those you care about and who are rooting for you, that something didn't get done. There's nothing like having to be accountable to others to up your game. Allowing others to help is hard, but it ultimately raises everyone's game, and suddenly that summit isn't nearly so far off.

Whenever it is possible, make sure you get your community involved. While it's possible to go solo, we recommend collecting a group of like-minded homeowners, business owners, and community members to aid in the push for sensible policies. This team of STR advocates should be made up of as many fellow homeowners and providers as possible, as well as groups who share a vested interest in the success of the short term rental economy.

Do a quick online search to see if there's a local short term rental alliance in your area – there may already be a push for regulations in full swing! We highly recommend getting as many people on board as possible. An advocacy group consisting solely of owners will naturally be viewed as biased, so you need a healthy combination of members from a diverse group of people.

You want local businesses and residents to tell the city that they vocally support and encourage the operation of vacation rentals. Also reach out to include your local tour operators as there are many local residents who are licensed tour operators. They'd be willing to spread the word about our investment for people willing to stay at local villages.

Sustainable Tourism

There was a time that few people would have considered remote areas as their holiday destination. With the improvement of technology and the globalization of the world, these things are gradually becoming a norm. Now tourism isn't limited to the main cities. People are discovering new paths and the need to explore has brought many people to consider these non-urban areas as the ideal holiday destination with Airbnb making it easier for local village entrepreneurs to reach out and invite the world to stay with them.

It is also the power of community that can help these rural areas create the best model to sustain non-urban tourism. The new option of Airbnb has finally put many villages on the map of the world as more and more travelers become aware of their existence. Airbnb is making it more convenient to gain a local perspective while guests stay there. A win-win in my book. It was at that time I finally felt that even these rural villages have that one major tool helping them better participate in the sharing economy and being more capable of becoming a part of sustainable tourism community.

This model is helping to create new economic opportunities where people live and is a great way of supplementing stagnated income. It wasn't until I talked to the people in villages during my travels that I realized the full extent of this move. The residents were grateful for the help that Airbnb's program had provided to them.

Infusion of Revenue

When Airbnb was considering this move, they began with a study that focused on measuring the economic impact and other significant effects of home-sharing in rural areas. The findings suggested that this move could enable the people living in rural areas and provide them a plethora of benefits. The study also answered the question that I had been wondering for a while... "Why should the traditional hospitality industry reap all the benefits of tourism?" The people in the countryside should also get their fair share of the benefits and the economic favors that non-urban tourism can bring. Many traditional hotel entrepreneurs cannot or will not service many of the smaller more rural off the beaten path villages leaving a void for the enterprising local entrepreneur willing to step up and change their fortunes.

As I was going through the report I came across the figures for 2016. The study found that for that year, the guest arrivals at non-urban listings amounted to a whopping 8.5 million. This is the proof that tourists are gradually turning their attention towards the destinations that aren't necessarily within the city limits.

As the rural communities have started welcoming more visitors, their stream of income has increased significantly. Airbnb allows the hosts to earn well without having to invest in expensive permanent infrastructures and it's not just in the report. I witnessed it first-hand. Many villagers will offer whatever space they have available at a reasonable price. It might not be much, but they genuinely want to share their home and lives with new people.

As I roamed around the villages, enjoying the local food, I could see the excitement in the area. Tourists were readily spending money on local food and souvenirs, and pretty soon that will have a significant impact on the economic stability of these rural places. With few opportunities to add an extra stream of income to their household, the convenient option of Airbnb is an easy way of earning. The report found that the income of non-urban Airbnb hosts for 2016 was $1.6 million, a significant increase over the past few years.

Summary

Airbnb is playing a part in solving the societal problems that hinder the success of rural areas. With effective investing and enterprising entrepreneurship, you too can reap the benefits of social impact investing. There was a time that I doubted the results of this move but with time I have become a believer.

My family just completed our latest full house rehab project in rural Central America. Using the support of our local NGO (Non-Governmental Organization) Non-Profit partner and residents we have our rustic rainforest retreat up and running. We are looking forward to receiving our first midterm rental guests very soon. We are excited to offer a unique and enjoyable retreat for guests and volunteers who will soon be experiencing what it's like to live in the rainforest and just how close, calm, serene and peaceful nature can be just outside your front door. Where the local villages are reaping the benefits of being hosts, their economic stability has also increased over time. The changes have started happening and gradually even bigger impacts will start to manifest.

At the start of the project fear could have controlled us and forced us to make irrational decisions but we proceeded with research, caution, understanding, information, experience, knowledge and faith. We thought long and hard about our investment theory, evaluated our lifestyle, came up with a game plan, acted and will soon be able to get some high returns; high returns that also make an impact on making the world a better place. All of this fueled and supported by the local community that we have built and supported throughout this adventure.

MATT MALOUF

Matt Malouf is a Part Time Investor and Author with a degree in Engineering from USC. His daytime gig is in Traffic Management focusing on technology integration and his part-time business niche is International Real Estate Investing, and Writing.

Matt Malouf has always been fond of writing and helping people. Over a course of some time, he gained the strength and courage to finally pursue another one of his dreams which led him to writing his first book to share personal experiences with his readers. Matt aims to enlighten the path his readers walk on and to learn lessons from his mistakes.

Matt Malouf has introduced value engineering problem-solving techniques to help people achieve their life goals and walk in the wake of success. He is a motivated individual who yearns to expand the horizons of his knowledge.

======

CONTACT:
You can read and review more of Matt's work at:
http://amazon.com/author/mattmalouf
Matt can be reached and consulted through his Clarity account at:
https://clarity.fm/mattmalouf

AFTERWORD

Thank you for taking the time to read through some stories and examples about how you can ignite the power of your community to achieve great success in your short-term rental business and in your life. Your community is always changing and ever evolving. It can be as big or as tight knit as you wish it to be, but the one thing your community should always share it a sense of belonging, love and support. We wish you all the best in your entrepreneurial ventures.

I envision this entire project to be eight volumes in total, if you would like to contribute to one or more of these volumes please reach out to me on my new Clarity page https://clarity.fm/mattmalouf and let's chat more. We live in the sharing economy today and part of that means sharing anything and everything we care to share, especially our life lessons and experiences. Personally, I found this project to be very inspiring and soul fulfilling, it was a lot of fun and I met some absolutely incredible people here. I believe we can all benefit and help each other on our journey to short term rental success by sharing our stories from the edge…. more to come, very soon! What do you have to share? More than you think, contact me today.

Be on the lookout for future volumes discussing women's entrepreneurship, expats moving abroad to set up a new life, investing in short term rentals, vacation rental markets, turbocharging your short-term rental business through renegade marketing techniques and of course regulations. See you soon.

www.ingramcontent.com/pod-product-compliance
Lightning Source LLC
Chambersburg PA
CBHW031553210526
45464CB00003B/1282